3/07

BIO
LAT

Queen Latifah

Simone Payment

The Rosen Publishing Group, Inc., New York

Published in 2006 by The Rosen Publishing Group, Inc.
29 East 21st Street, New York, NY 10010

Library of Congress Cataloging-in-Publication Data

Payment, Simone.
Queen Latifah / by Simone Payment.—1st ed.
    p. cm.—(The library of hip-hop biographies)
Includes bibliographical references (p.) and index.
ISBN 1-4042-0518-7 (library binding)
1. Latifah, Queen—Juvenile literature. 2. Rap musicians—United States—Biography—Juvenile literature. I. Title. II. Series.

ML3930.L178P29 2006
782.421649'092–dc22

                                                    2005020329

Manufactured in the United States of America

On the cover: Queen Latifah performs in Los Angeles, California, in August 2005.

CONTENTS

INTRODUCTION

Queen Latifah wears many crowns. She's a Grammy Award–winning rapper and an Academy Award–nominated actress. She's also been a successful businesswoman, author, talk-show hostess, and model. From learning how to rap in her friend's basement, Queen Latifah has managed to build a one-woman media empire. She continues to succeed at everything she tries.

Queen Latifah is quick to point out that her success is the result of hard work. As she wrote in an introduction to *Stay Strong: Simple Life Lessons for Teens* by Terrie Williams, "I wasn't born in a recording studio, or running a business, or on the set of a popular television show. The CDs and the TV programs weren't just given to me. It took years and years of hard work and relentless dedication to get where I am today."

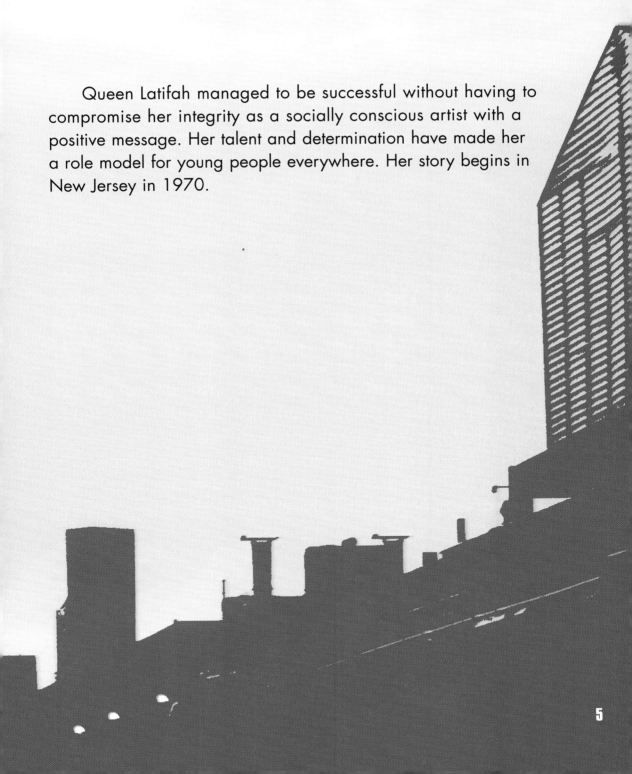

Queen Latifah managed to be successful without having to compromise her integrity as a socially conscious artist with a positive message. Her talent and determination have made her a role model for young people everywhere. Her story begins in New Jersey in 1970.

CHAPTER ONE

DIFFERENT FROM THE START

Queen Latifah's father, Lance Owens Sr., was a police officer and a Vietnam veteran. Her mother, Rita Bray Owens, took care of their home and kept busy raising Queen Latifah's brother, Lance Owens Jr., who was born two years before Queen Latifah.

In the introduction to Queen Latifah's autobiography, her mother says, "From the beginning I knew my daughter was going to be different." Born on March 18, 1970, she was "eight pounds, three ounces [3.7 kilograms], with a mind of her own." Her parents named her Dana Elaine Owens.

EARLY LIFE

"I think I was born independent," Queen Latifah said in an interview in *Essence* magazine. As a baby, she was very active and always exploring. She refused to wear the frilly clothes her mother tried to dress her in. Instead, she was a tomboy, always trying to keep up with her brother and his friends. Lance Jr. and Dana were very close, and they loved to play basketball and board games together.

When Dana was eight years old, she decided to choose a Muslim name for herself. Dana's cousin Sharonda had a book that

The movie *Beauty Shop* had its premiere in Los Angeles, California, on March 24, 2005. Queen Latifah, who starred in the movie, is seen here with her mother and father at the premier. Queen Latifah's parents had a huge influence on her growing up, and she recognizes that their support and positive influence helped her get where she is today.

listed Muslim names and what each name meant. As soon as Dana saw the name Latifah, she knew it was perfect for her. It means "delicate, sensitive, and kind" and that's exactly what she was—on the inside. On the outside she was tough and independent.

That same year, her parents separated. Lance Jr. and Queen Latifah moved with their mother to Hyatt Court, a housing project in a rough neighborhood in Newark, New Jersey. At first, their mother struggled to support them. She worked two jobs so she could save enough money for a better apartment. At the same time, she went to college so she could fulfill her dream of becoming a teacher.

Despite the long hours and difficulty of juggling school and work, Queen Latifah's mother always made sure she had time to spend with the children. She made their apartment safe and comfortable, and the family had dinner together every night. She made sure Queen Latifah had the music and dance lessons she wanted. She even managed to send her daughter to private school until she was a sophomore in high school.

MUSIC RUNS IN THE FAMILY

Queen Latifah's parents were a big influence on her when she was growing up. She was proud of what her mother accomplished, and she respected her father who, as a police officer, was always helping people. She also got her love of music from her parents. Her mother and father had been in choirs and small singing groups when they were teenagers. Later in his life, Queen Latifah's father ran a jazz club in Newark. He also sang and played the drums.

Every summer, Queen Latifah and her brother would go south to Virginia and Maryland to visit their mother's relatives.

Having been a star power forward on her high school basketball team, Queen Latifah plays for charity in MTV's second annual Rock 'N Jock B-Ball Jam in 1992. The proceeds of the event went to help children with AIDS (acquired immunodeficiency syndrome). Queen Latifah donates time and money to numerous charities, and has even established one herself.

There, Queen Latifah would sing in their aunt's church choir. During the rest of the year, Queen Latifah sometimes sang in the choir at the Shiloh Baptist Church in Bloomfield, New Jersey.

HIGH SCHOOL

Queen Latifah's teenage years were not always easy. At that time, there weren't many role models for girls her size, and she struggled with the fact that she was taller and bigger than many of her friends. She sometimes wrote poetry as a way of dealing with her feelings.

As a sophomore, Queen Latifah transferred to Irvington High School in Irvington, New Jersey, where her mother had gotten a job teaching art. Queen Latifah was a good student at Irvington. Popular and outgoing, she played power forward on the girls' championship basketball team. In her senior year, she won four awards given by her fellow students: Most Popular, Most Comical, Best Dancer, and Best All Around.

Although she didn't sing in her school choir, Queen Latifah had occasional roles in school plays and musicals. She played the part of Dorothy in her school's production of *The Wiz*. She also sang "If Only for One Night" by Luther Vandross in a school talent show. Before she went onstage, she was very scared. In her autobiography, she remembers that she couldn't breathe and "broke out into an instant sweat at the thought of going out in front of all those people." Queen Latifah was afraid they wouldn't like her singing. To overcome her fear, she decided to focus on the positive and assume that they would like her. Her confidence paid off. She got a standing ovation, and next time she wasn't so scared.

In addition to her schoolwork, basketball, and singing, Queen Latifah worked at Burger King. At closing time on Saturdays, after a long shift behind the counter or cleaning tables, she would quickly change out of her Burger King uniform

BEATBOXING

Besides rapping with Ladies Fresh, Queen Latifah also served as a human beatbox. Beatboxers use their mouths to produce rhythms for MCs to rap over. Depending on the skill of the beatboxer, these rhythms can sound like a simple drumbeat or a whole collection of instruments. Beatboxing was invented in New York by hip-hop artists such as Doug E. Fresh and Buff the Human Beatbox of the Fat Boys. Beatboxing is less popular today than it was in the 1980s, but it is beginning to make a comeback with artists such as Rahzel.

and stuff it into her backpack. Then she would head to Latin Quarters, a hip-hop club in New York City. Queen Latifah was in love with hip-hop, and by her junior year of high school she had joined forces with two of her friends—Tangy B and Landy D— to form a rap group called Ladies Fresh. Ladies Fresh became popular, performing frequently for their friends at Irvington and winning a school talent contest. Queen Latifah was on her way to becoming a famous rapper.

CHAPTER TWO

A RAPPER BECOMES A QUEEN

When Queen Latifah was in high school, hip-hop music was on the rise. The first hip-hop song to become popular across the United States was called "Rapper's Delight." It was by a group called the Sugar Hill Gang and came out in 1979. Soon rappers like Grandmaster Flash and Kurtis Blow followed with hits of their own.

Although hip-hop started out as a small cultural movement in New York City, its influence spread quickly. By the middle of the 1980s, hip-hop music was popular in many parts of the United States.

Break dancing came out of New York City around the early 1970s and soon became an essential part of hip-hop culture, along with graffiti, MCing, and DJing. Originally known as b-boying, break dancing involves acrobatic dance moves. In this photo from the early 1980s, a young man performs in Manhattan's Washington Square Park.

Elements of hip-hop culture such as break dancing, graffiti, and hip-hop fashion also gained national attention.

MORE THAN JUST MUSIC

Queen Latifah wanted to be a part of the hip-hop scene. In her autobiography, she emphasizes that hip-hop is more than just music. It is "an expression, a culture, an attitude." Hip-hop gave kids a platform to voice their opinions and talk about what was

WOMEN IN HIP-HOP

Women have been involved in hip-hop music since it first emerged in the late 1970s. Sha Rock, one of the first female MCs, started rapping as a teenager in the Funky 4 + 1. Roxanne Shante was the first female MC to score a hit single, recorded when she was only fourteen years old. The 1984 song, called "Roxanne's Revenge," sold more than 250,000 copies in New York City alone.

Queen Latifah was heavily influenced by MC Lyte, one of hip-hop's earliest and most outspoken feminists. A pioneering, socially conscious rapper, MC Lyte would go on to contribute to antiviolence campaigns and AIDS charities. Queen Latifah was also influenced by Salt-N-Pepa, a trio of two female MCs and a female DJ named Spinderella. Salt-N-Pepa was the first all-female hip-hop group, and the trio's catchy songs and tough attitude brought its members mainstream success.

MC Lyte performs at the 2004 BET Awards ceremony. She has been releasing records since she was twelve years old. She was the first female rapper to receive a gold record for album sales.

going on in their lives. Queen Latifah realized that hip-hop could be more than just entertainment—it could be used to spread a positive message.

In a 2005 interview with a British newspaper, Queen Latifah said that in high school she "lived and breathed hip-hop." She came back from Latin Quarters every weekend with tapes of the music she had heard. She also brought hip-hop styles and slang back with her to her New Jersey high school. She said that "right in front of my eyes, the new era of hip-hop was being born—Grandmaster Flash, Salt-N-Pepa, Beastie Boys— I watched them grow, and they inspired me."

Most of the performers Queen Latifah saw at Latin Quarters were men. But a few, including DJ Jazzy Joyce and Sweet Tee, were women. They became role models for Queen Latifah. When she saw them performing onstage, she started to believe that someday she could be onstage, too.

A HIP-HOP EDUCATION

Queen Latifah's friends also loved hip-hop, and they would become very important to her career. DJ Mark the 45 King spun records at parties at Irvington High School. Queen Latifah's mother knew Mark because she helped organize school activities. She introduced her daughter to DJ Mark, and they became friends.

Queen Latifah and some of her friends began hanging out in Mark's basement in East Orange, New Jersey, where they met other young rappers. They listened to the latest music and studied hip-hop magazines such as *Right On!* and *Word-Up*. In her autobiography she says, "We wanted to know everything we could about the artists, the music, the clothes. We studied rap inside and out." The people who hung out in Mark's basement began calling themselves the Flavor Unit, and some of them eventually got record deals. Queen Latifah says their success may have been because "we were so prepared: we knew what we were getting ourselves into. It was like training before the job."

While hanging out in Mark's basement, Queen Latifah practiced rapping. At first she wasn't very good, but her friend Ramsey persuaded her to keep working at it. As her skills improved, Queen Latifah began to realize that she could be a rapper. "I knew I had it in me," she says in her autobiography. "I could hear in my head the way I wanted it to sound. It was just a matter of getting it from my brain to my voice."

Although Queen Latifah loved hip-hop, she didn't think she could make a career out of it. She wanted to be a lawyer or a newscaster. After graduating from Irvington High School, she began classes at Borough of Manhattan Community College.

EARLY SUCCESS

While in college, Queen Latifah began to think about putting out a record. After all, some of her friends from the Flavor Unit had gotten record deals. Her friend Ramsey believed that Queen Latifah could get one, too. He gave her $700—his rent money for the month—to make a demo. She and DJ Mark used the money to go to a recording studio in Orange, New Jersey. There they recorded two songs: "Wrath of My Madness" and "Princess of the Posse."

Fab Five Freddy is a seminal figure in the world of hip-hop. Freddy began his career as a graffiti artist when he was still a teenager. He would go on to be the first VJ to host MTV's *Yo! MTV Raps*, the first television show to feature hip-hop music videos. He also starred as himself in the 1982 film *Wild Style*, a movie about the early New York City hip-hop scene.

DJ Mark gave the demo to Fab Five Freddy, a former graffiti artist who was the host of the hit show *Yo! MTV Raps*. Fab Five Freddy liked the demo so much that he gave it to Dante Ross, who worked at Tommy Boy Records. It wasn't long before Queen Latifah's phone rang. Someone from Tommy Boy was on the line, asking her whether she wanted to record an album.

Tommy Boy offered Queen Latifah a record deal in 1988. When she signed the contract, Tommy Boy asked her what name she wanted to use on her records. She decided that

Queen Latifah strikes a pose for the camera in this 1989 photograph. Her distinctive look and sound marked Queen Latifah as a true original, and it wasn't long before success found her. One year after making her demo with DJ Mark the 45 King, she was already embarking on a European tour in support of *All Hail the Queen*. Although she wasn't yet out of her teens, Queen Latifah was already a star.

Latifah was too plain. She thought about calling herself Princess of the Posse. Instead, she decided to add "Queen" to her name because it made her feel strong, proud, and important.

After she chose her stage name, Tommy Boy gave Queen Latifah money to buy clothes to wear in photos for posters and album covers. She wanted something that would set her apart. She went to a clothing store in downtown Newark and bought an African print top. She had a seamstress at the store make her pants to match. Because she couldn't find shoes to go with her new outfit, she went barefoot in photos and onstage during her concerts. The crowds at her concerts loved her look, and they loved her music. Queen Latifah was about to become a star.

CHAPTER THREE

QUEEN OF THE CHARTS AND SCREEN

Shortly after getting her record deal, Queen Latifah started recording the songs that would appear on her first album. She also began a tour of the United States and Europe. All of this work left little time for school, and Queen Latifah left college. Her mother wasn't too happy about this, but she knew that Queen Latifah was a smart, confident young woman. She believed in her daughter's abilities, so she gave Queen Latifah the freedom to pursue her dream.

ALL HAIL THE QUEEN

Throughout 1989, Queen Latifah continued to work on her first album. It was hard work, but DJ Mark was in the studio to help her. Not many female rappers had been successful at that point, so Tommy Boy didn't want to spend much money recording the album. At the time, Queen Latifah didn't think about the fact that she was one of only a few female hip-hop artists. She told the *Chicago Sun-Times*, "[I] thought about doing my own thing and making my own album. It didn't really faze me that there weren't a lot of women in the business or that the women that were around didn't look like me."

All Hail the Queen came out in 1989. Despite her record company's fears, the album was very successful, especially for a debut album. It sold more than a million copies and went to number six on *Billboard*'s hip-hop/R & B chart. (*Billboard* is a music magazine that keeps track of record sales and ranks records.) *All Hail the Queen* was also a success with music critics. The album got good reviews and was nominated for a Grammy Award. Although she didn't win, the nomination was a huge honor for someone who wasn't even twenty years old yet.

New versions of Queen Latifah's first demos, "Princess of the Posse" and "Wrath of My Madness," were included on the album. Queen Latifah also recorded a duet called "Ladies First" with fellow female rapper Monie Love. With this song, Queen Latifah and Monie Love said that it was important for women to

Queen Latifah, seen here performing a song in Los Angeles, California, was on top of the world in 1990. She had won numerous awards for *All Hail the Queen*, which many critics considered to be one of the best hip-hop albums ever released. Her tour in support of the album, which began in 1989, was rewarded as an unequaled success. Barely out of high school, Queen Latifah was already receiving popular and critical acclaim.

respect themselves and to demand respect from others. In her autobiography, Queen Latifah says, "I had something to say to everybody in my music. But I decided to address the ladies first. We have the power to set the men straight."

Another song on *All Hail the Queen*, called "Evil That Men Do," featured the rapper KRS-One. "Evil That Men Do" addressed societal problems such as drugs, homelessness, and violence.

The New Music Seminar, a music convention held every year in New York City, gave Queen Latifah its Best New Artist award in 1990. She also won Best Female Rapper in *Rolling Stone* magazine's reader's poll. Although Queen Latifah's music career was just beginning, she was already being rewarded for her work.

NATURE OF A SISTA

Tommy Boy released Queen Latifah's second album, *Nature of a Sista*, in 1991. *Nature of a Sista* was more stylistically diverse than *All Hail the Queen*, branching out into reggae, dance music, and even jazz. *Nature of a Sista* was successful, but did not sell as many copies as *All Hail the Queen*. Despite this, *Nature of a Sista* was a strong record. The album starts out with the furious "Latifah's Had It Up 2 Here," which became a hit. The album also contains tracks on which Queen Latifah sings, something that she would do with increasing frequency throughout her career.

In addition to recording music and touring, she started a company called Flavor Unit Management and Records in 1991. She appointed herself chief executive officer, which means that she was the head of the company. Shakim Compere, one of her friends from the days when she would hang out in DJ Mark's basement, became her business partner. Queen Latifah's mother also worked at Flavor Unit.

Flavor Unit found new hip-hop acts and helped them get started in the music business. One of the most successful acts that Queen Latifah and her company discovered was Naughty

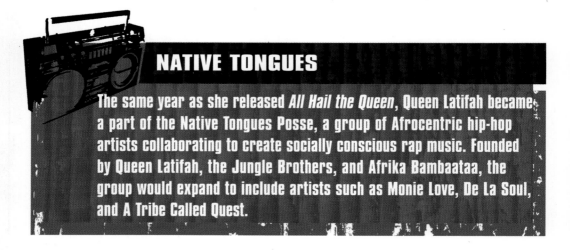

NATIVE TONGUES

The same year as she released *All Hail the Queen*, Queen Latifah became a part of the Native Tongues Posse, a group of Afrocentric hip-hop artists collaborating to create socially conscious rap music. Founded by Queen Latifah, the Jungle Brothers, and Afrika Bambaataa, the group would expand to include artists such as Monie Love, De La Soul, and A Tribe Called Quest.

by Nature. Naughty by Nature became extremely popular, and its first two singles sold more than 1 million copies each.

TRAGEDY STRIKES

Everything was going well for Queen Latifah in early 1992. She was on tour, and her song "Latifah's Had It Up 2 Here" was a hit. In addition, she got her first movie role, a small part in the Spike Lee film *Jungle Fever*. Her business was thriving and she had just bought a house where she, her mother, and her brother could all live together. Then one night a phone call changed everything. Her friend Ramsey called and told her that her brother, Lance Jr., had been in a motorcycle accident. Queen Latifah rushed to the hospital, where her mother was waiting. After a few hours, a doctor came out of the operating room to give them the bad news. Lance Jr. was dead.

One of Flavor Unit Management's most successful discoveries was a young hip-hop outfit known as Naughty by Nature, whose members were from Queen Latifah's home state of New Jersey. Flavor Unit got the group a record deal with Tommy Boy, and its 1991 single, "O.P.P.," became a nationwide radio hit. Naughty by Nature poses with Queen Latifah in this photograph from the 1995 Soul Train Music Awards.

Queen Latifah was devastated by Lance Jr.'s death. She couldn't believe he was gone. They had been close growing up and remained close as young adults. One of their favorite things to do together was ride motorcycles. Queen Latifah had bought Lance Jr. the motorcycle he was riding when he got into the accident. She still has the key to the motorcycle, which she wears around her neck to remind her of her brother.

After Lance Jr. died, Queen Latifah began to do drugs and drink heavily. For months she walked around as if she were in a fog. Finally, she realized that she should be strong for her brother. Using alcohol and drugs wouldn't bring him back or help her cope with her loss. For help dealing with Lance's death, Queen Latifah went to a counselor.

MUSIC HELPS EASE THE PAIN

Music also helped Queen Latifah deal with her brother's death. A few months after he died, she began recording her third album, *Black Reign*.

Black Reign came out in 1993 and was another huge success for Queen Latifah. The album featured smart, socially conscious lyrics, and sold more than 500,000 copies. Guest rappers on the album included Heavy D and KRS-One. In the song "U.N.I.T.Y.," Queen Latifah tells men to respect women, and tells women to stand up to men and respect themselves. "U.N.I.T.Y." won a Grammy Award for Best Rap Solo Performance. Queen Latifah was proud of the album and the hard work she put in to make it a success.

The final song on *Black Reign* is called "Winki's Theme." It is about Lance Jr., who was nicknamed Winki. (As a baby he blinked a lot and it seemed as though he were winking at people.) Queen Latifah dedicated the album to her brother, and it had a picture of Lance Jr.'s grave on the cover.

QUEEN LATIFAH'S DISCOGRAPHY

All Hail the Queen, 1989
Nature of a Sista, 1991
Black Reign, 1993
Order in the Court, 1998
She's a Queen: A Collection of Hits, 2002
The Dana Owens Album, 2004

LIVING SINGLE

After *Black Reign* came out, Queen Latifah decided to put her music career on hold and turn her attention to acting. By this time she had been in a number of movies, including *House Party 2*, *Juice*, and *My Life*. She had also made some guest appearances on television shows like *The Fresh Prince of Bel-Air*, which starred the rapper Will Smith.

Her acting career really took off in 1993, however, when she was cast in a major role on a new television show called *Living Single*. Queen Latifah played Khadijah James, a young woman who had started her own magazine. Khadijah shared a New York apartment with her cousin and a friend. *Living Single* was a huge success and stayed on the air for several years.

Living Single aired on Fox from 1993 to 1998 and made Queen Latifah a household name. Extremely popular during its five-year run, *Living Single* received two NAACP Image Awards.

Fox wanted to cancel the show in 1997, but so many loyal fans wrote and called the network that Fox brought it back for another year.

Queen Latifah moved to Los Angeles, California, after joining the cast of *Living Single*. Although her career was still skyrocketing, she began to have some problems in her personal life. In July 1995, Queen Latifah went to the Apollo Theater in Harlem, New York, with some friends. On the drive home, she pulled over to wait for her friends' car to catch up. While she was stopped, two men came up to the car and told her they'd shoot her if she didn't get out. Although she and her bodyguard Shawn did what they said, the carjackers shot Shawn in the stomach. Queen Latifah quickly got help. After surgery at a local hospital he recovered. Queen Latifah was later able to identify the carjackers, and they were arrested and convicted.

The next year, Queen Latifah was stopped for speeding in Los Angeles. She admitted to the policeman who stopped her that she had a gun and some drugs in the car. Queen Latifah told *Entertainment Weekly* magazine that she had the gun with her because she was still afraid from her carjacking a year earlier. She also said that the arrest was "really embarrassing. I was just really worried about [how it would affect] my family." Queen Latifah pleaded guilty to the charges against her, and she was put on probation for two years.

QUEEN OF THE SILVER SCREEN

Queen Latifah appeared in a number of movies and television shows during the years she was acting in *Living Single*. She starred in the 1996 movie *Set It Off*, which was about four African American women who were bank robbers. She played a bank robber named Cleo, one of her most challenging roles, and she earned great reviews for her performance. In 1997, she was given two awards for her role in the movie. She won Best Actress at the Black Film Awards and Best Supporting Actress at the Independent Film Awards.

Queen Latifah thought that the good reviews she got for *Set It Off* would lead to parts in other movies. She did get a lot of offers, "but they weren't good," she told *Entertainment Weekly* magazine. "There was nothing I could really do about it. I had to wait for the better material . . . [I]t was good I had *Living Single* to fall back on." Rather than lower her standards, she decided to hold out for a good offer.

Her patience finally paid off when she was offered a part in the 1998 movie *Living Out Loud*. In the movie, Queen Latifah

Set It Off, a story about a group of friends who become bank robbers in Los Angeles, California, was a huge success at the box office. This still shows the friends (from left to right: played by Jada Pinkett Smith, Kimberly Elise, Queen Latifah, Vivica A. Fox) celebrating after pulling off a heist. Queen Latifah was nominated for an Independent Spirit Award for her portrayal of Cleo, which she considers one of her favorite roles.

plays a lounge singer who performs classic jazz and blues songs. Although audiences knew she was a great rapper, she surprised many people with her fantastic singing. Queen Latifah got good reviews for the job she did in *Living Out Loud.* Roger Ebert, a movie critic at the *Chicago Sun-Times,* said that "her screen presence makes a scene stand up and hum."

ORDER IN THE COURT

With *Living Single* off the air and *Living Out Loud* completed, Queen Latifah turned her attention back to music. In 1998, she put out an album called *Order in the Court*. The album had a heavy soul and R & B influence, and guest stars included Pras from the Fugees and R & B singer Faith Evans. Queen Latifah revisits her brother's death in the song "What Ya Gonna Do." Another song ("Life") is about the deaths of Tupac Shakur and the Notorious B.I.G. Although *Order in the Court* was not quite as successful as her earlier albums, it did well. Queen Latifah would now take a six-year hiatus from making music—and she would be busier than ever.

CHAPTER FOUR

THE QUEEN MOVES IN MANY DIRECTIONS

With her success in music, television, and movies, Queen Latifah was building an impressive career. In 1998, she appeared in a TV miniseries called *Mama Flora's Family* and in the movie *Sphere*. In 1999, her autobiography, *Ladies First: Revelations of a Strong Woman*, was published. Focusing mostly on her life away from the stage and screen, *Ladies First* is filled with sharp observations about life and a positive message for young and old readers alike. That same year, she appeared alongside Denzel Washington and Angelina Jolie in the movie *The Bone Collector*.

During his 2000 presidential campaign, Democratic candidate Al Gore stopped by the *Queen Latifah Show*. She made a point of showing the audience that, no matter how famous her guests were, they were just normal, everyday people. Although her talk show only ran for two years, it was a learning experience for Queen Latifah and brought her a great deal of mainstream success.

While working on the movie she received a lot of valuable career advice from her costar Denzel Washington.

That September, Queen Latifah went in yet another direction. Encouraged by her friend Rosie O'Donnell, Queen Latifah decided to host her own talk show. The guests on her show included celebrities ranging from Snoop Doggy Dogg to Al Gore, as well as regular people with everyday problems. She hosted the *Queen Latifah Show* for three seasons, and it was hard work.

THE AWARDS PILE UP FOR *CHICAGO*

For her portrayal of Mama Morton in *Chicago*, Queen Latifah won a Black Reel Award and a Screen Actors Guild Award. She was also nominated for a British Academy of Film and Television Arts (BAFTA) Award, a Golden Globe, a Teen Choice Award, and an MTV Movie Award.

CHICAGO

When her talk show ended, Queen Latifah returned to acting. Director Rob Marshall was working on a movie version of the popular musical *Chicago* and Queen Latifah wanted to be in it. She wanted to play the role of Mama Morton, who runs a women's prison. Queen Latifah faced some stiff competition for the part, and had to audition three times before she got it. When auditioning, she "had a touch of nervousness but not 'I can't do this.' I never take a job I don't think I can do," she told *Entertainment Weekly* magazine.

Not only did Queen Latifah get the part, it ended up being her most successful movie role to date. In 2002, when *Chicago* was released, Queen Latifah won praise for both her singing and her acting. In addition, she also became the first female rapper to be nominated for an Academy Award. She was nominated for Best Actress in a Supporting Role, and although she did not win, Queen Latifah still felt extremely honored to get the nomination.

More movie appearances followed. Queen Latifah was in *Scary Movie 3* and *Barbershop 2,* and was the voice of Cha-Cha in *The Country Bears.* She also produced and starred in *Bringing Down the House* with Steve Martin and Eugene Levy. *Bringing Down the House* came out in 2003, and Queen Latifah wore many hats in getting it to the screen. In addition to producing and starring in the movie, she also worked on the script and helped choose the other cast members.

Chicago, released in 2002, was an adaptation of the 1975 Broadway musical of the same name. Queen Latifah played the prison warden Mama Morton in the movie, receiving critical praise and an Academy Award nomination. She starred alongside Catherine Zeta-Jones, Richard Gere, and Renée Zellweger.

A NEW DIRECTION IN MUSIC

While she was working on the movie *Taxi* (released in 2004), Queen Latifah began to record another album. After a hard day on the movie set, she would go straight to the recording studio. She told the *Philadelphia Inquirer* that it wasn't easy to do both at the same time, but recording was relaxing. "Being on a

Queen Latifah performs the song "Lush Life," originally written by jazz pianist and composer Billy Strayhorn, at the forty-seventh annual Grammy Awards in 2005. Besides performing, Queen Latifah also hosted the event. *The Dana Owens Album* was nominated for best vocal jazz album, and although she did not win an award, receiving the nomination was a great honor.

movie set is work, plain and simple. So going to the studio after that is like going to the beach . . . Even if I showed up tired, I was energized there."

For her next record, she used her real name. *The Dana Owens Album* came out in 2004 and shows another side of Queen Latifah. This album is a collection of songs Queen Latifah listened to while she was growing up. She had sung some of these songs in the movie *Living Out Loud* and had wanted to record more for a long time. The album sold well and was nominated for a Grammy. Although she still considers herself a hip-hop artist, she wanted to show people that she was more than just a rapper. "I came to a point where the beats and rhymes were too small to contain me. There was more to say," she told the *Philadelphia Inquirer*.

Queen Latifah has also recorded a new rap album, but it had not been released at the time of this writing. She told *USA Today* that many of the songs on the album have a positive message, something that she feels is missing in rap music today. In her autobiography, Queen Latifah writes, "As a rapper, I've learned that what you put out in the spoken and in the written word is what you'll get back. That's why I keep my music positive. I want to uplift, I want to inform."

In addition to writing and recording new music, Queen Latifah is continuing her movie career. The movie *Beauty Shop* was released in 2005. Queen Latifah not only stars in the movie, she also helped raise the money needed to make it. She's always looking for new movie projects and would rather look for them than wait for them to come to her. "I love being able to take an idea and sell it to a [movie] studio," she told *USA Today*.

LIFE OUTSIDE THE SPOTLIGHT

When Queen Latifah has free time, she enjoys driving one of her many cars, motorcycles, and scooters. She would like to have children sometime soon and would also like to adopt children. Queen Latifah gives her time and money to causes she thinks are important. She does charity work for children's groups, AIDS research, and women's sports. After her brother's death, Queen Latifah and her mother started a scholarship fund in his name. Each year, the Lancelot H. Owens Scholarship Foundation gives money to minority high school students who need help financing their education. Students from all over the United States can apply. Winners must agree to help their community, as Queen Latifah's brother did when he was a policeman.

Queen Latifah spends as much time as she can with her friends and family. She still has a home in New Jersey, close to her parents. Her mother works for Flavor Unit, and her father manages security for her. Queen Latifah says that her parents and her friends have kept her from letting her success go to her head. She told *Ebony* magazine that when she visits her mother, she has to take out the garbage and walk the dog. She says that being nominated for an Academy Award "means nothing when . . . you gotta pick up poop behind your momma's doggie."

A ROLE MODEL FOR EVERYONE

Queen Latifah has appeared in ads for CoverGirl cosmetics and has modeled for the Lane Bryant clothing store. Although she may have a glamorous image, it's more important to Queen Latifah that she is pretty on the inside. She urges young girls not to pay attention to the way society tells people they should look. In her autobiography she says, "You shouldn't want to look like anyone but you." She goes on to say, "Each of us has a queen inside. It starts by feeling good about yourself. A queen . . . is proud of who she is, whether she is a corporate executive or a cleaning lady."

Queen Latifah has gotten to the top by working hard, being smart, making good choices, and being good to the people around her. In the introduction to the 2001 book *Stay Strong: Simple Life Lessons for Teens*, Queen Latifah tells teens that they can do what she has done. She writes, "You can do whatever you want to do, be whatever you want to be, and be a success. *If* you work hard at whatever you do and really look inside yourself and decide that you want to be a good person."

Queen Latifah is a strong woman with a strong message. In addition to her many other roles, we can add one more: teacher.

TIMELINE

1970   Queen Latifah is born (given name: Dana Elaine Owens) on March 18.

1989   Queen Latifah releases her first record, *All Hail the Queen*.

1991   Queen Latifah releases her second record, *Nature of a Sista*.

1993   Queen Latifah is nominated for a Grammy Award for Best Rap Solo Performance ("Latifah's Had It Up 2 Here").
She releases her third record, *Black Reign*.

Her television show *Living Single* debuts on Fox TV.

1995   Queen Latifah wins a Grammy for Best Rap Solo Performance ("U.N.I.T.Y.").

1996   Queen Latifah appears in the film and on the soundtrack for *Set It Off*.

1997   Queen Latifah wins the Aretha Franklin Award for Entertainer of the Year at the 1997 Soul Train Lady of Soul Awards.

1998   Queen Latifah releases her fourth record, *Order in the Court*.

She appears in *Living Out Loud*.

1999 Queen Latifah's talk show debuts.

Her book, *Ladies First: Revelations of a Strong Woman,* is published.

She appears in *The Bone Collector.*

2002 Queen Latifah releases a greatest hits album, *She's a Queen: A Collection of Hits.*

2003 Queen Latifah produces and stars in *Bringing Down the House.*

The cast of *Chicago* wins a SAG Award for Best Cast Performance.

2004 Queen Latifah wins an NAACP Image Award for Outstanding Actress in a Motion Picture *Bringing Down the House.*

She releases her fifth record, *The Dana Owens Album.*

2005 Queen Latifah hosts the Grammy Awards
She stars in *Beauty Shop.*

GLOSSARY

autobiography The story of a person's life, written by that person.

contract A legal agreement to do something, signed by two people or two groups.

demo A rough recording that a musician makes to demonstrate what he or she sounds like.

hiatus A break or interruption.

housing project A group of low-cost houses or apartment buildings opened by a government agency.

Muslim A person who follows the religion of Islam.

nominate To choose as a candidate for a special honor.

ovation Enthusiastic applause.

record deal A contract between an artist and a recording company.

record label A company that signs musicians to a contract and then records, releases, and publicizes their music.

seamstress A woman who makes clothes.

single A specific song from a record album that is released separately from the album.

FOR MORE INFORMATION

Interscope Records
2220 Colorado Ave.
Santa Monica, CA 90404
(310) 865-1000
Web site: http://www.interscope.com

Web Sites

Due to the changing nature of Internet links, the Rosen Publishing Group, Inc., has developed an online list of Web sites related to the subject of this book. This site is updated regularly. Please use this link to access the list:

http://www.rosenlinks.com/lhhb/qula

FOR FURTHER READING

Bloom, Sarah R. *Queen Latifah*. Philadelphia, PA: Chelsea
    House Publishers, 2002.

Haskins, Jim. *One Nation Under a Groove*: Rap Music and Its
    Roots. New York, NY: Jump at the Sun, 2000.

Jones, Maurice K. *Say It Loud!: The Story of Rap Music*. New
    York, NY: Millbrook Press, 1994.

Madden, Annette. *In Her Footsteps: 101 Remarkable Black
    Women from the Queen of Sheba to Queen Latifah*.
    Berkeley, CA: Conari Press, 2000.

Tracy, Kathleen. *Queen Latifah*. Hockessin, DE: Mitchell Lane
    Publishers, 2005.

Williams, Terrie. *Stay Strong: Simple Life Lessons for Teens*. New
    York, NY: Scholastic, 2001.

BIBLIOGRAPHY

Ascher-Walsh, Rebecca. "Queen Victorious as Oscar Gives Her the Royal Treatment." *Entertainment Weekly*, March 7, 2003.

Baraka, Rhonda, and Gail Mitchell. "Lady Rappers: How Three TCB." *Billboard*, December 7, 2002.

Bloom, Sarah R. *Queen Latifah*. Philadelphia, PA: Chelsea House Publishers, 2002.

Ebert, Roger. "Living Out Loud." *Chicago Sun-Times*, November 6, 1998. Retrieved June 2, 2005 (http://rogerebert.suntimes.com/apps/pbcs.dll/article?AID=/19981106/REVIEWS/811060301/1023).

Freydkin, Donna. "Queen Latifah Is Stylin'." *USA Today*, March 29, 2005. Retrieved May 25, 2005 (http://www.usatoday.com/life/people/2005-03-29-latifah_x.htm).

Kim, Jae-Ha. "Another Jewel for Her Crown," *Chicago Sun-Times*, January 13, 1999. Retrieved June 2, 2005 (http://www.jaehakim.com/articles/books/features/queen2.htm).

Marisa, Fox. "Queen Latifah Lets Loose." *InStyle*, March 1, 2005.

Moon, Tom. "Latifah: Queen Bee of Multitalented Musicians." *Philadelphia Inquirer*, September 30, 2004.

Norment, Lynn. "Queen Latifah Changes Her Figure and Her Tune." *Ebony*, January 2005.

"Queen Latifah." *Contemporary Black Biography,* Vol. 16. Henderson, Ashyia N., and Ralph G. Zerbonia, eds. Farmington Hills, MI: Thomson Gale, 1997.

Queen Latifah with Karen Hunter. *Ladies First: Revelations of a Strong Woman.* New York, NY: William Morrow, 1999.

"Queen Latifah." *Notable Black American Women,* Book II. Smith, Jessie Carney, ed. Farmington Hills, MI: Thomson Gale, 1996.

Rose, Tiffany. "Queen Latifah: Having It Large." *The Independent*, April 26, 2005. Retrieved May 25, 2005 (http://enjoyment.independent.co.uk/music/interviews/story.jsp?story=633131).

Tracy, Kathleen. *Queen Latifah.* Hockessin, DE: Mitchell Lane Publishers, 2005.

White, Evelyn C. "The Poet and the Rapper." *Essence*, May 1, 1999.

Williams, Terrie. *Stay Strong: Simple Life Lessons for Teens.* New York, NY: Scholastic, 2001.

INDEX

About the Author

Simone Payment has a degree in psychology from Cornell University and a master's degree in elementary education from Wheelock College. She is the author of twelve books for young adults. Her book *Inside Special Operations: Navy SEALs* (also from Rosen Publishing) won a 2004 Quick Picks for Reluctant Young Readers award from the American Library Association and is on the Nonfiction Honor List of Voice of Youth Advocates.

Photo Credits

Cover, pp. 1, 13, 17 © Getty Images, Inc.; p. 7 © Michael Germana/ The Everett Collection; p. 9 © Ron Galella/WireImage.com; p. 14 © Michael Caulfield/WireImage.com; p. 18 © Al Pereira/The Michael Ochs Archive; p. 22 © Neal Preston/Corbis; p. 25 © Trapper Frank/Corbis Sygma; p. 28 © The Everett Collection; p. 30 © Corbis Sygma; p. 33 © Reuters/ Corbis; p. 35 © Miramax/courtesy the Everett Collection; p. 36 © AFP/ Getty Images, Inc.

Designer: Thomas Forget